panic cord

Words & Music by Jez Ashurst, Gabrielle Aplin & Nicholas Atkinson

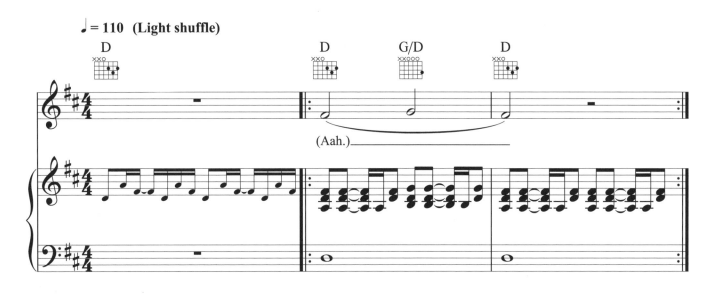

(Aah.)

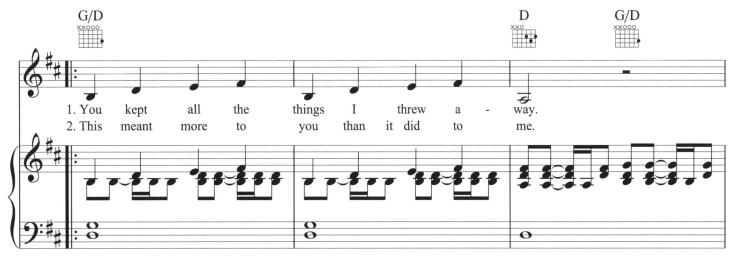

1. You kept all the things I threw a - way.
2. This meant more to you than it did to me.

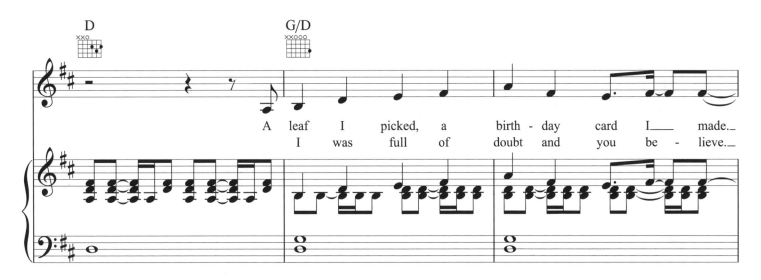

A leaf I picked, a birth - day card I __ made. __
I was full of doubt and you be - lieve. __

© Copyright 2013 Major 3rd Music Limited.

Universal Music Publishing Limited/BMG Rights Management (UK) Limited/Stage Three Music Publishing Limited.

All Rights Reserved. International Copyright Secured.

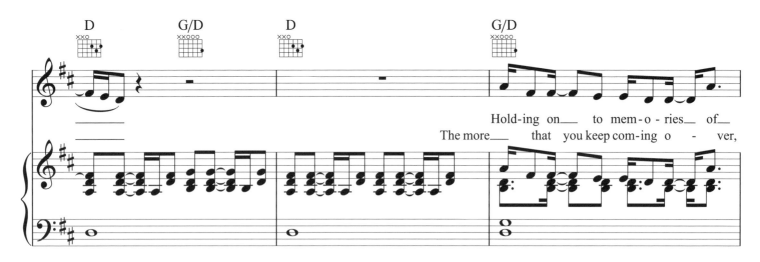

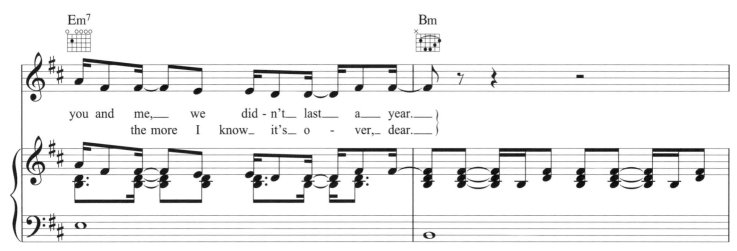

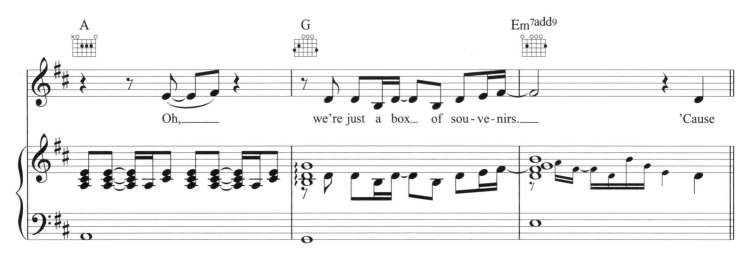

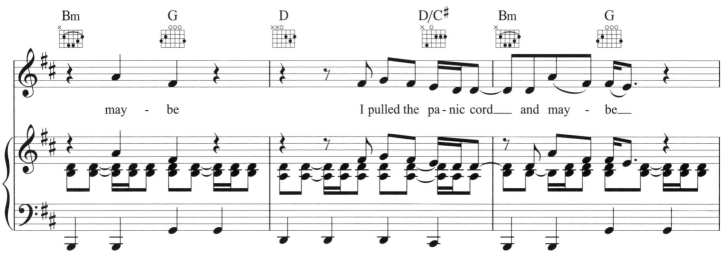

you were hap-py, I___ was bored.___ May-be I want-ed you___ to change.___

May-be I'm the one___ to blame.___

May - be_____ you were just__ too nice__ to me___ and may-be

it took me way__ too long___ to leave. May-be once___ we felt___ the same.___

keep on walking

Words & Music by Nicholas Atkinson & Gabrielle Aplin

© Copyright 2013 Universal Music Publishing Limited/Stage Three Music Publishing Limited.
All Rights Reserved. International Copyright Secured.

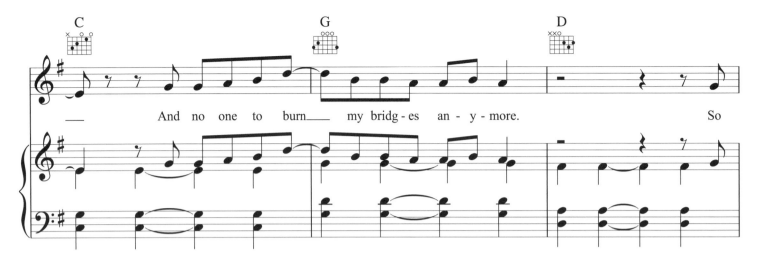

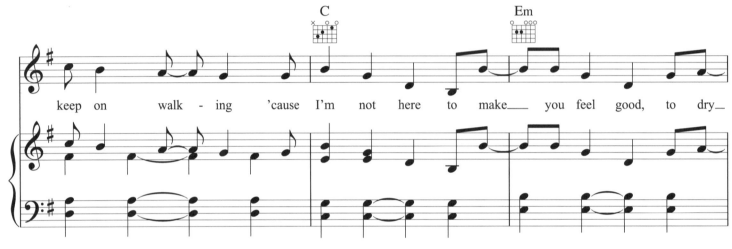

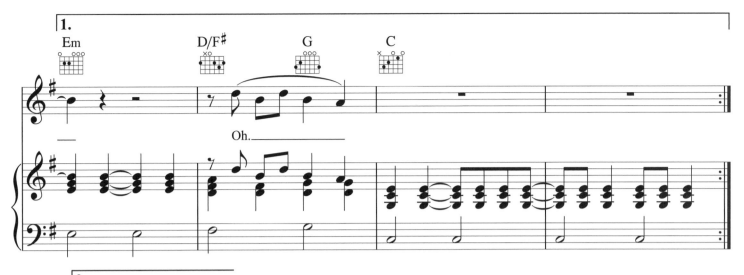

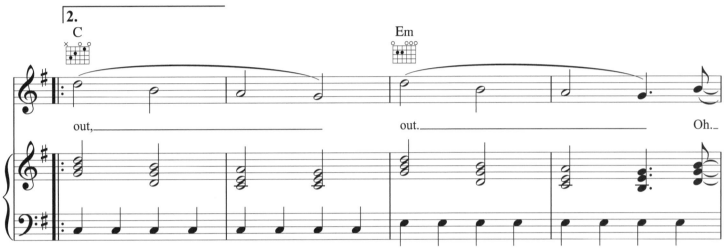

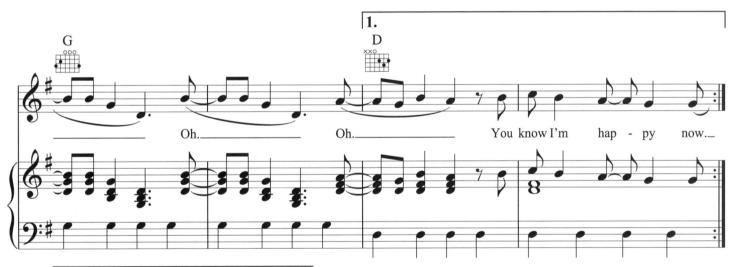

please don't say you love me

Words & Music by Nicholas Atkinson & Gabrielle Aplin

†Symbols in parentheses represent chord names with respect to capoed guitar.
Symbols above represent actual sounding chords.

© Copyright 2013 Universal Music Publishing Limited/Stage Three Music Publishing Limited.
All Rights Reserved. International Copyright Secured.

2. Heav-y words___ are hard_ to take, un-der pres - sure pre-cious things

can break.__ And how we feel___ is hard to fake,___ so let's not give_

___ the game_ a - way.___

D.S. al Coda

Just

Coda

F
(C)

D⁷/F♯
(A⁷/C♯)

___ And fools___ rush in.___ And I've been the fool___ be - fore.___

15

look at me___ like that___ And there's no need to wor-

-ry when___ you see just where___ we're at___ Just please don't say you love___

___ me 'cause I might___ not say it back.___ Just

please don't say you love___ me 'cause I might___ not say it back.___

how do you feel today?

Words & Music by Nicholas Atkinson & Gabrielle Aplin

© Copyright 2013 Universal Music Publishing Limited/Stage Three Music Publishing Limited/Peermusic (UK) Limited.

All Rights Reserved. International Copyright Secured.

20

how do you feel to - day?

How do you_____ feel to -

-day?   'Cause to - night I'm clos - ing

all the doors____ so stay out - side or lay down with our flaws.____

I knew your sto - ries, I knew it was love._____

But those songs and bells_____ were laugh-ter of___ guns._____

D.S. al Coda

So

Coda

23

home

Words & Music by Nicholas Atkinson & Gabrielle Aplin

© Copyright 2013 Universal Music Publishing Limited/Stage Three Music Publishing Limited.

All Rights Reserved. International Copyright Secured.

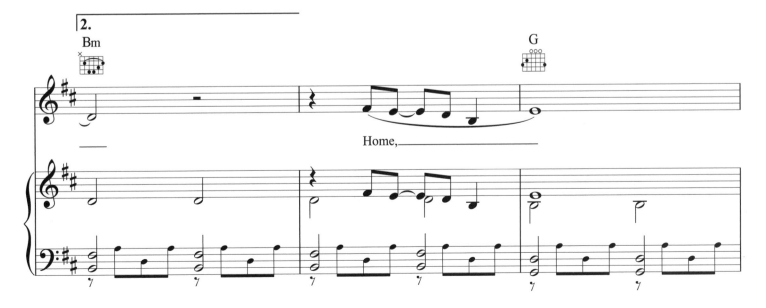

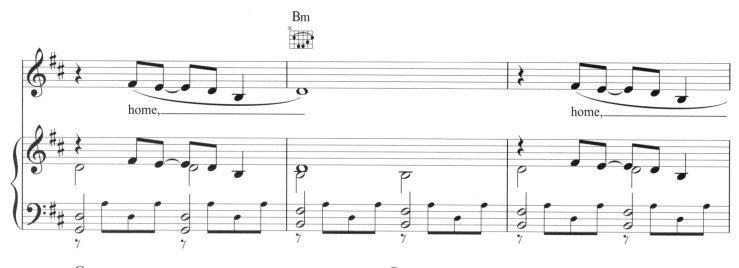

home,_____

home,_____

_____ home._____ 'Cause they say

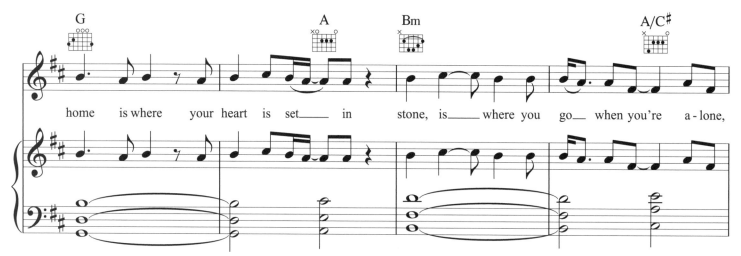

home is where your heart is set_____ in stone, is_____ where you go__ when you're a-lone,

is where you go__ to rest__ your bones._____ And it's

Salvation

Words & Music by Joel Pott & Gabrielle Aplin

© Copyright 2013 Universal Music Publishing Limited/Chrysalis-Music-Limited.
All Rights Reserved. International Copyright Secured.

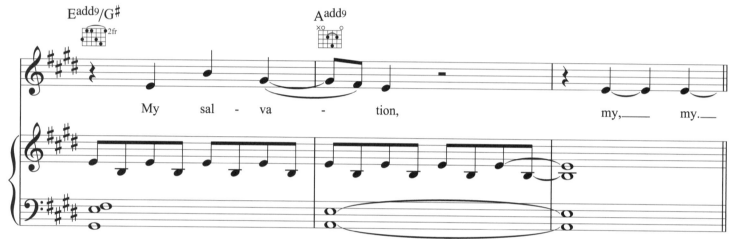

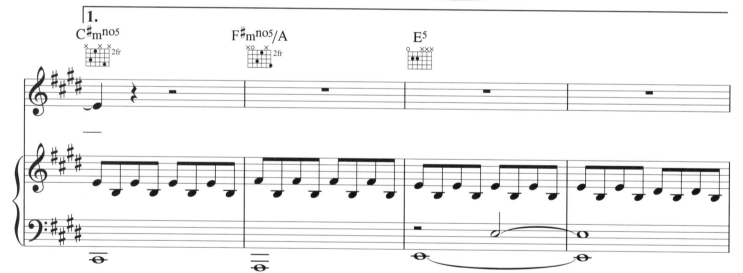

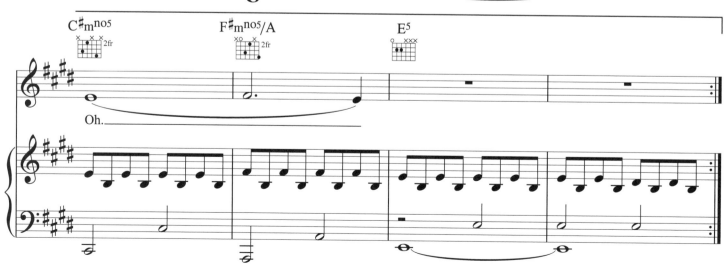

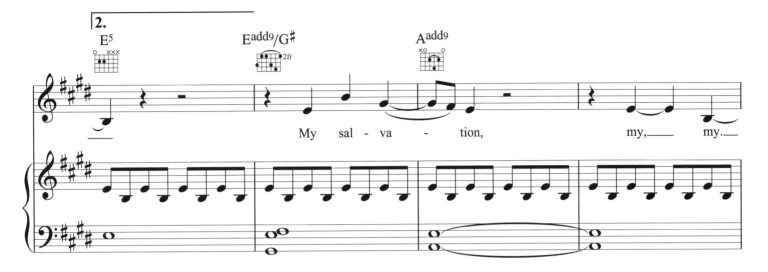

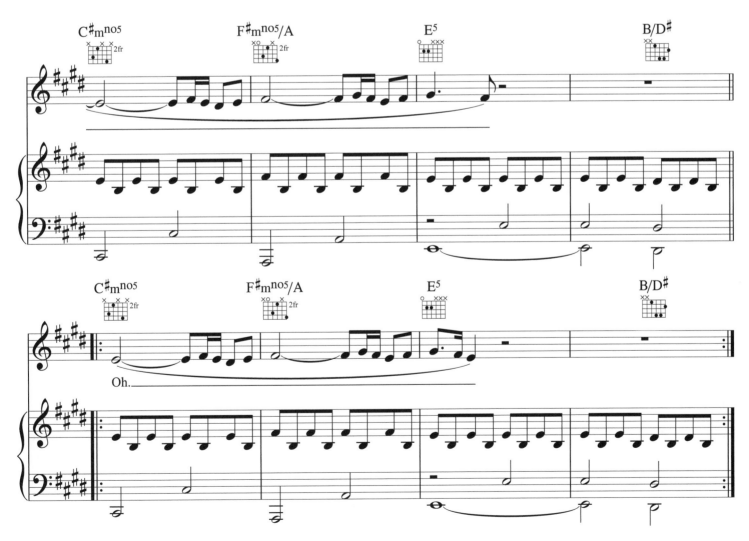

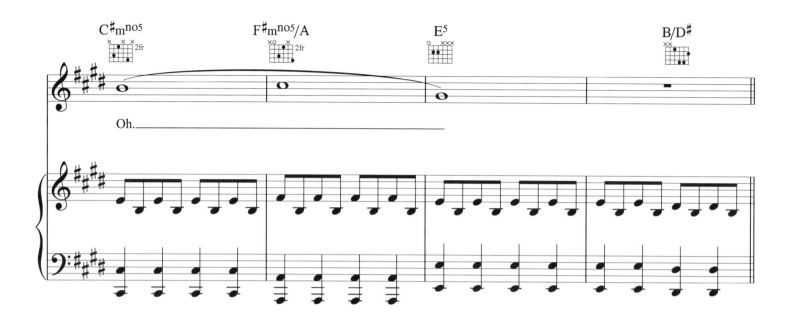

Oh._____

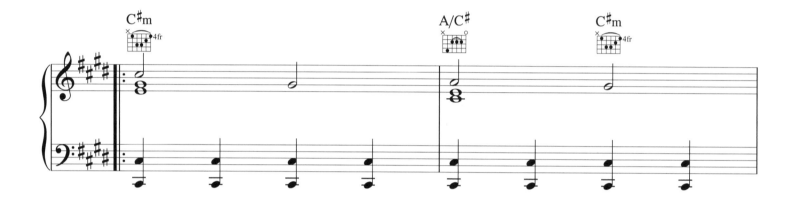

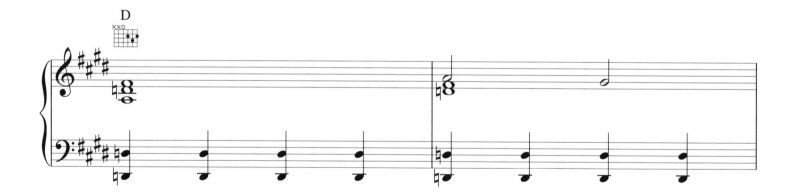

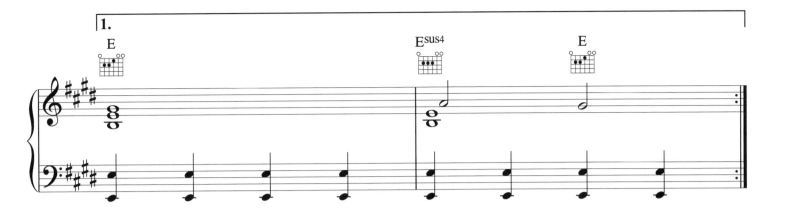

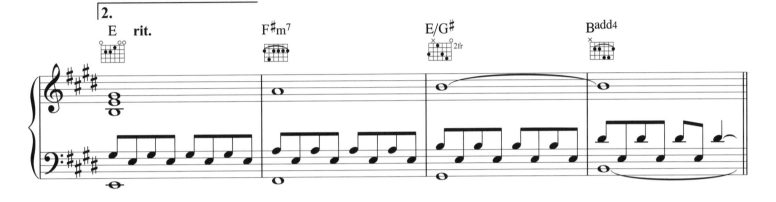

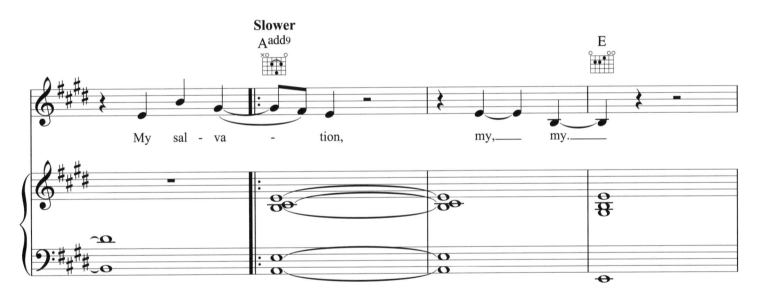

My sal - va - tion, my,____ my.____

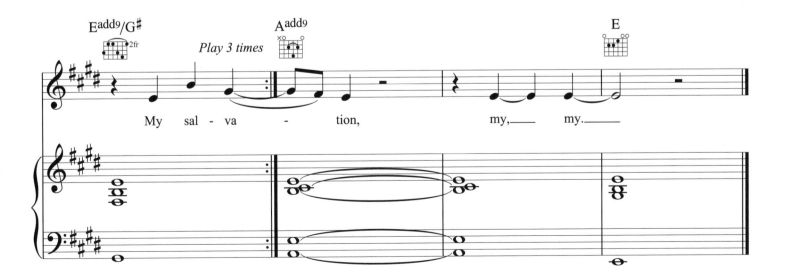

My sal - va - tion, my,____ my.____

ready to question

Words & Music by Nicholas Atkinson, Gabrielle Aplin & Thomas Wilding

1. Is there some-thing I'm not___ see - ing?___ Some-thing you're not tell - ing

© Copyright 2013 Universal Music Publishing Limited/Stage Three Music Publishing Limited/Peermusic (UK) Limited.
All Rights Reserved. International Copyright Secured.

Oh._____ Read - y to ques - tion, oh,_____

___ that life is a bless - ing, oh._____

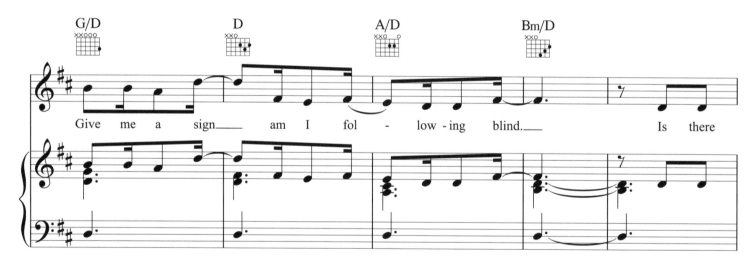

Give me a sign___ am I fol - low - ing blind.___ Is there

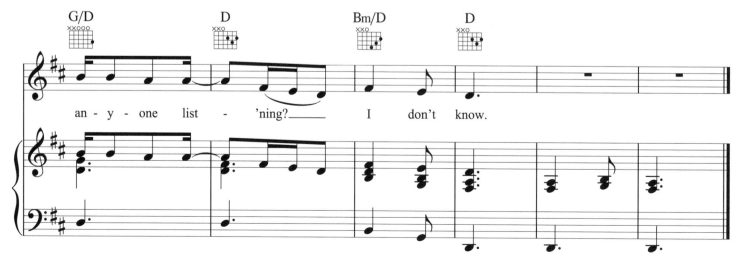

an - y - one list - 'ning?_____ I don't know.

the power of love

Words & Music by Holly Johnson, Mark O'Toole, Peter Gill & Brian Nash

© Copyright 1984 Perfect Songs Limited.

All Rights Reserved. International Copyright Secured.

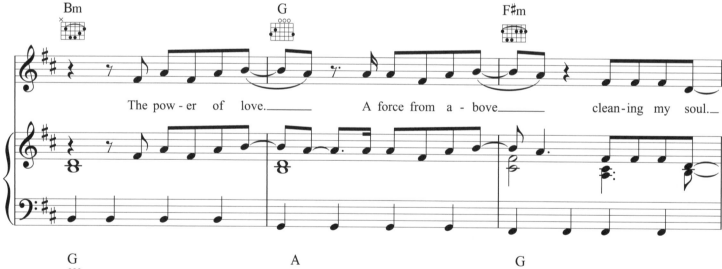

Purge the soul. Make love your goal.

2. I'll pro-tect you from the hood-ed claw, keep the vam-pires from your door.

When the chips are down I'll be a-round with my un-dy-ing

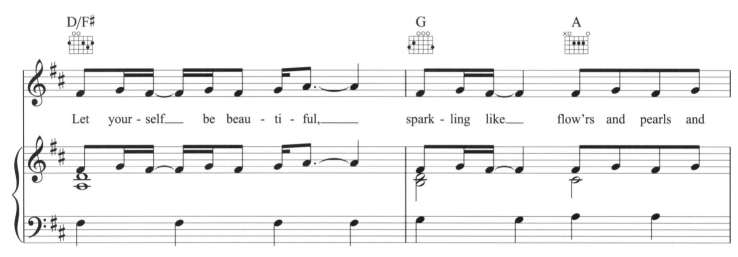

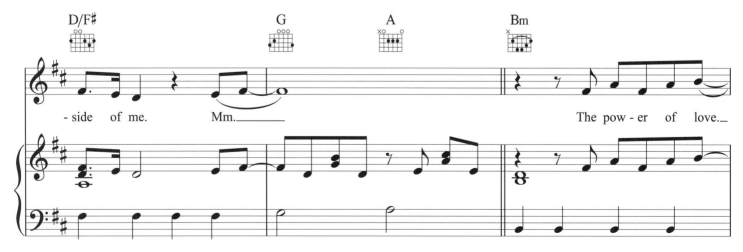

dan - ger,___ love is plea - sure. Love is pure, the on - ly trea - sure.___ I'm___ so in

love with you. Make love your___ goal.___

The pow - er of love.___ A force from a - bove___

clean - ing my___ soul.___ The pow - er of love._

alive

Words & Music by Gabrielle Aplin & Michael Spencer

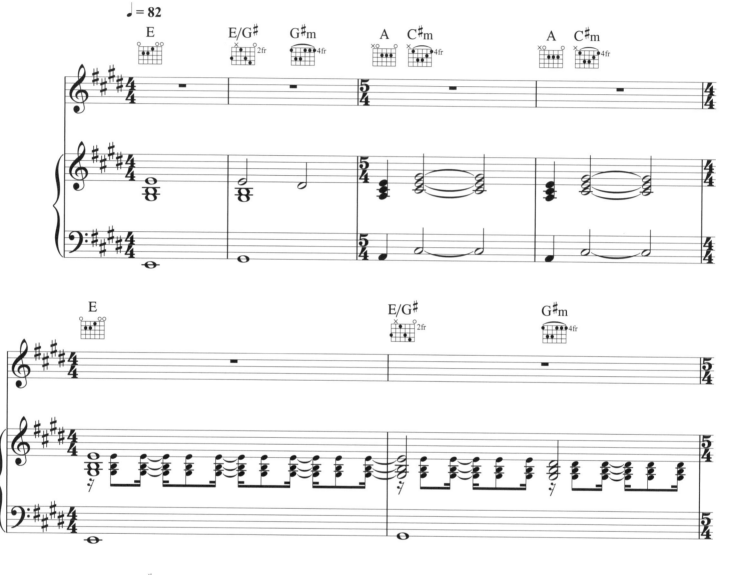

1. Just_

© Copyright 2013 Universal Music Publishing Limited/Copyright Control.

All Rights Reserved. International Copyright Secured.

48

re - al - ise_____ you have to

1.

feel a - live._____ All your

wor - ries will e - scape_ through the door.___ And you'll

wake up___ all a-lone on___ the floor.___ It's not too late,_____

just re - ly on me now. 2. Nine

2.

feel a - live in -

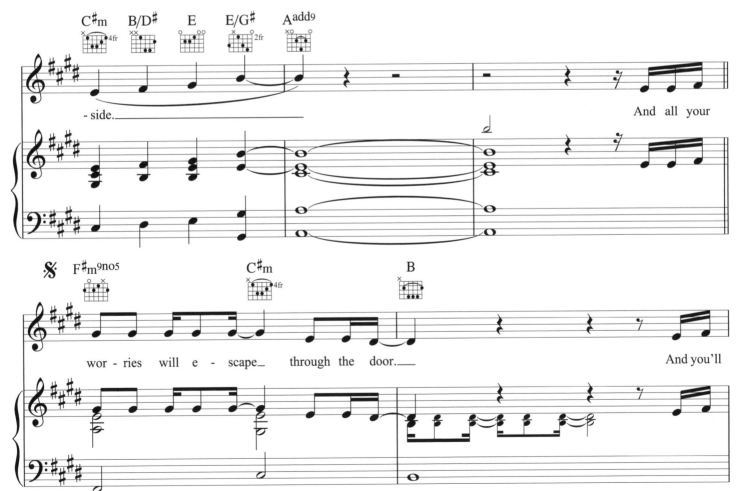

- side. And all your

wor - ries will e - scape through the door. And you'll

wake up___ all a-lone on___ the floor.___ It's not too

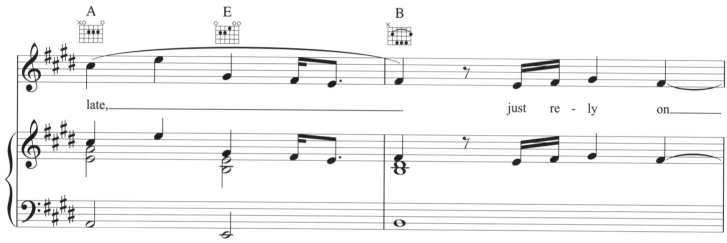

late,___ just re - ly on___

To Coda

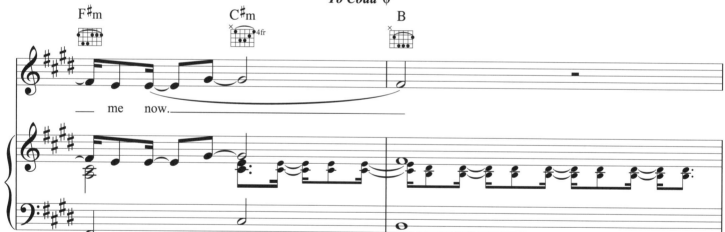

___ me now.___

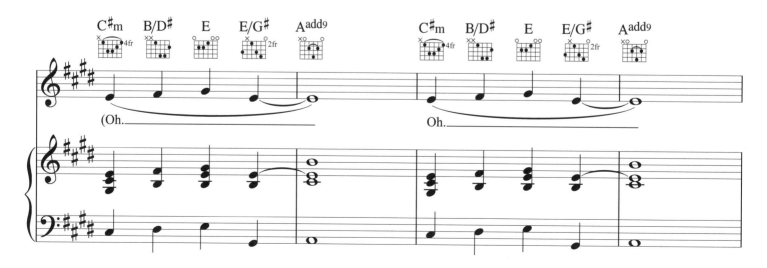

(Oh.___

Oh.___

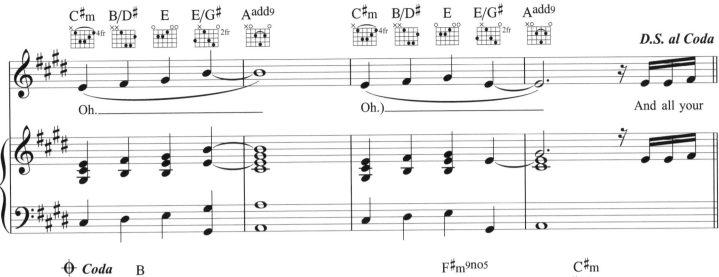

D.S. al Coda

Oh. _____ Oh.) _____ And all your

Coda

All your wor-ries will e-scape through the door.___

And you wake up___ all a-lone on___ the floor._____ It's not too

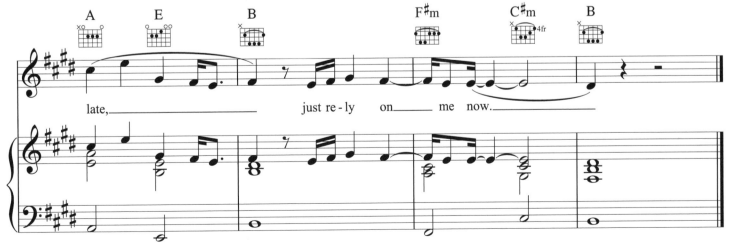

late,_____ just re-ly on___ me now._____

human

Words & Music by Nicholas Atkinson, Gabrielle Aplin & Thomas Wilding

†Symbols in parentheses represent chord names with respect to capoed guitar.
Symbols above represent actual sounding chords.

© Copyright 2013 Universal Music Publishing Limited/Stage Three Music Publishing Limited/Peermusic (UK) Limited.
All Rights Reserved. International Copyright Secured.

56

november

Words & Music by Luke Potashnick & Gabrielle Aplin

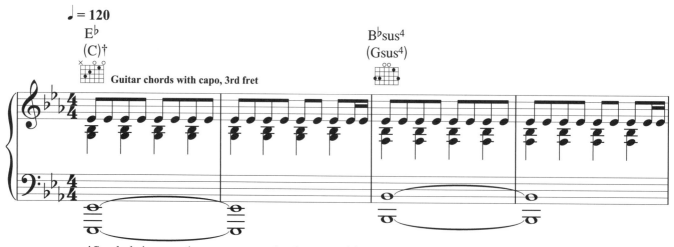

†Symbols in parentheses represent chord names with respect to capoed guitar.
Symbols above represent actual sounding chords.

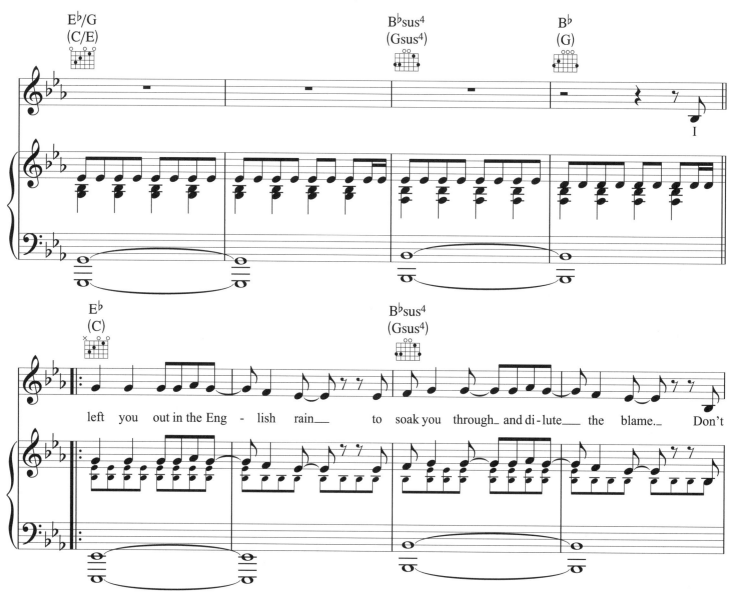

left you out in the Eng - lish rain__ to soak you through__ and di - lute__ the blame.__ Don't

© Copyright 2013 Blue Sky Music Limited

Universal Music Publishing Limited/Sony/ATV Music Publishing.

All Rights Reserved. International Copyright Secured.

but now it al-ways floods with rain._____ Oh,_____ how can I for-give?_____ Those_____ words will stain for - ev - er. I

I al-ways used__ to love__ No - vem - ber

start of time

Words & Music by Jim Irvin, Julian Emery & Gabrielle Aplin

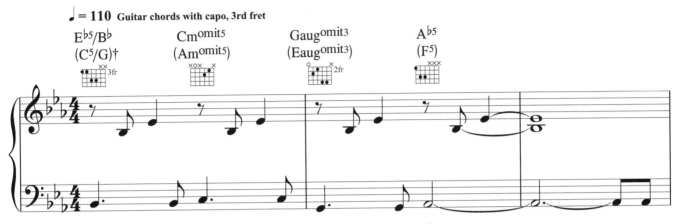

†Symbols in parentheses represent chord names with respect to capoed guitar.
Symbols above represent actual sounding chords.

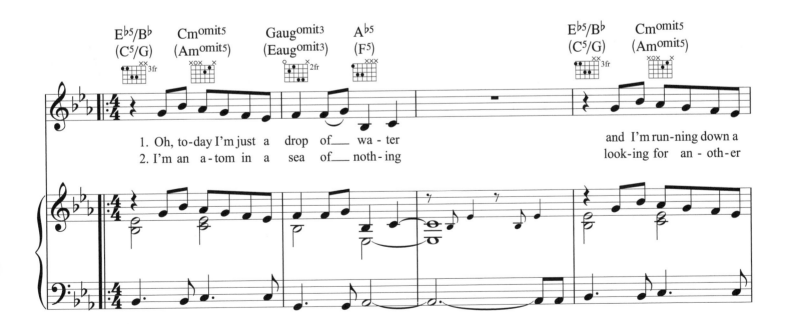

1. Oh, to-day I'm just a drop of___ wa-ter and I'm run-ning down a
2. I'm an a-tom in a sea of___ noth-ing look-ing for an-oth-er

© Copyright 2013 Warner/Chappell Music Publishing Limited/Universal Music Publishing Limited.
All Rights Reserved. International Copyright Secured.

moun-tain - side._____

to com - bine._____

Come to-mor-row I'll be in the__ o - cean,

May-be we could be the start of__some-thing,

I'll be ris - ing with the morn - ing tide.

be to-geth - er at the start of time.

There's a ghost up-on the moor to - night,

now it's in our house._____

When you walked in - to the room just then

it's like the

out.   It's like the sun came out.

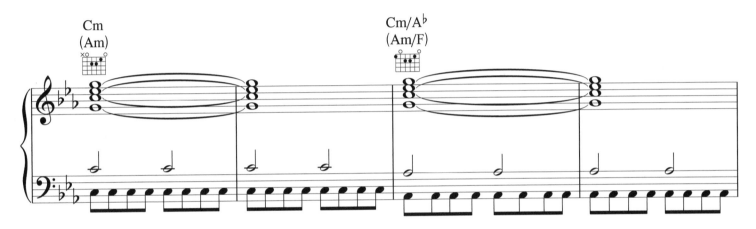

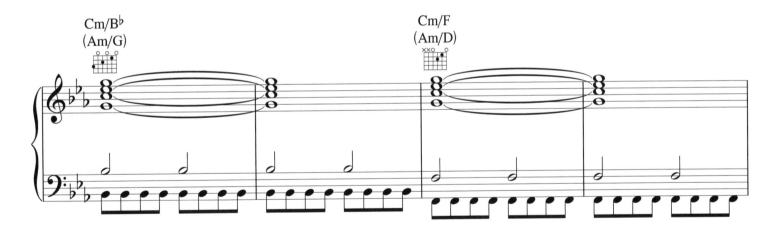

Fade

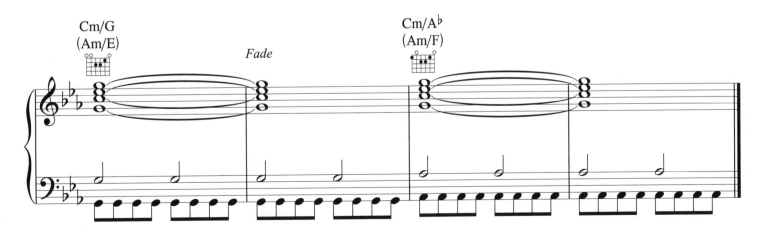

take me away

Words & Music by Gabrielle Aplin

© Copyright 2013 Universal Music Publishing Limited.
All Rights Reserved. International Copyright Secured.

in a sea of self - in - flic - tion that I felt.
dis - con - nect - ed from the things I love the most.

1. **2.**

2. My

You've seen my best turn to the worst, I've dragged you right down with me.

Want to con - fess but with the stress I'm scared you'll leave me. Now I

want you to know,— but you can take it on— your— own.—

I am hol-low, I am numb,— I am

star - ing down the bar - rel of this— gun.— I am al - ways by my - self,—

— in a sea— of self - in - flic - tion that I— felt.—

123456789